Alfred Lambourne

The Old Journey

Reminiscences of Pioneer Days

Alfred Lambourne

The Old Journey
Reminiscences of Pioneer Days

ISBN/EAN: 9783744744300

Printed in Europe, USA, Canada, Australia, Japan

Cover: Foto ©Andreas Hilbeck / pixelio.de

More available books at **www.hansebooks.com**

The Old Journey

Reminiscences
of
Pioneer Days

By
ALFRED LAMBOURNE

GEO. Q. CANNON & SONS CO
Publishers

Preface.

The author is one of those who "crossed the plains," an achievement which at the time did not seem great in its inception nor mighty in its accomplishment, so crowded with pleasurable incidents was the journey and so full of the inspiration aroused by the necessities and ambitions of the undertaking were all. As the years have gone, however, and time has not only cast a sort of glamour over the event, but has given men an opportunity to reflect thoughtfully and in calmness and intelligence, that same journey assumes greatness in our eyes, both in inception and in its achievement. It finds a prominent place in the history of the nation, and will ever stand forth among great events. Indeed, the world had theretofore seen nothing like it, and in the very nature of things

PREFACE

its repetition is improbable if not impossible. It must now be read; it cannot be experienced.

Some years ago the author was enabled to gratify an ambition to record in artistic form something of the scenes and something of the memorable Westward March: ("An Old Sketch Book," Boston. S. E. Cassino, 1892). The purpose was not to publish a guide-book of the plains, for which there has been no occasion within the present generation, but rather an epitome, a poetic-prose narration of a typical journey, as seen through the memory, and devoid of commonplaces, the more salient features only looming through the past.

When the Jubilee Celebration of the strange journey—for it is that and those who made it that we are this year commemorating and honoring—was decided upon, it was suggested that an appropriate souvenir of the occasion would be "The Old Sketch Book." That work, however, was a large and costly volume of a limited edition, and hardly manageable for the present purpose. The author

PREFACE

therefore decided to place the matter and sketches in the form now used, under the title of " The Old Journey," and carefully revised and lengthened the descriptive portions. The prompting to undertake the work was not merely encouraging but was made almost a duty by the commendations of the original volume. These commendations were not confined to the press alone, which, however, was liberal in its notice and approvement, but were given orally and through the pen. Had there been no other result of his labors, the author would have felt fully repaid for them by the expressions of approbation from those who saw the birth of the State and who have watched its growth to the present hour.

It was in consideration of the singular fitness of "The Old Journey" as a souvenir to be presented, during the Jubilee, to the Pioneers still living, that the following letters were addressed to the Pioneer Jubilee Celebration Commission and they speak for themselves. Many of the names

PREFACE

appended to the letters will at once be recognized as belonging to the honored band of Pioneer men and women, while the others are of those who think that in this Jubilee Year, both those who crossed the plains by ox-teams and those that came later in palace cars will desire and appreciate a work of this character.

To the Honorable Utah Pioneer Jubilee Commission,

Ladies and Gentlemen:

We, the undersigned citizens of Utah, respectfully suggest that a very pleasant feature of the celebration to be given under your direction would be the presentation to each of the Pioneers of 1847, of a copy of that beautiful work of art by Alfred Lambourne, "The Old Journey, Reminiscences of Pioneer Days." If the Commission will purchase, say five hundred copies of this unique and excellent work, for presentation as it may decide, we are of the opinion that it will be highly

PREFACE

appreciated by the Pioneers, and be fully endorsed by the public, as it certainly will be by

Yours Respectfully,
Wilford Woodruff,
Thomas G. Webber,
Wm. B. Preston,
Geo. Q. Cannon,
Brigham Young,
L. S. Hills,
Charles W. Penrose,
Henry Dinwoodey,
John T. Caine,
Lorenzo Snow,
James Sharp,
W. W. Riter,
George Romney,
John Henry Smith,
M. H. Walker,
C. C. Goodwin,
Heber J. Grant,
Heber M. Wells.

PREFACE

To the Honorable Utah Pioneer Jubilee Commission,

Ladies and Gentlemen:

We, the undersigned women of Utah, (some actual pioneers of 1847) are intensely interested in a new book, now in the hands of the publishers, by the well-known author and favorite home artist, Mr. Alfred Lambourne.

Appreciating the efforts the writer has made heretofore, we can safely recommend "The Old Journey, Reminiscences of Pioneer Days," which is the title, and we know the entire work will be, in every respect, superior in excellence of design and workmanship, and a home production.

As a work of art, it will be worth preserving, and as an ideal souvenir of that memorable pilgrimage from the borders of civilization to the Great American Desert, will be a most unique gift to the venerable Pioneers who yet remain with us.

Therefore we respectfully suggest to the Com-

PREFACE

mission, that it purchase a suitable number of these books for presentation.

Zina D. Young,
Elmina S. Taylor,
Bathsheba W. Smith,
Emmeline B. Wells,
M. Isabella Horne,
Jane S. Richards,
Romania B. Pratt,
Annie Taylor Hyde,
Anne C. Woodbury,
Mary A. C. Lambert,
Sarah J. Cannon,
Mary Hyde Wolf,
Zina Young Card,
Maria L. Nebeker,
Lucy B. Young,
Eurithe K. La Barthe,
Rosina Godbe,
Priscilla P. Jennings,
M. B. Salisbury.

In presenting this edition there are no excuses to offer. The author has been true to nature and to history, and the publishers have done their part in

PREFACE

a manner that must excite wonder and commendation when one thinks of what has been achieved in the wilderness within the few years that have passed since the sketches appearing in this book were made.

It is but proper to acknowledge, and it is done with gratitude, that except for the kind and generous assistance of the following well-known citizens of the State, neither the original work nor this Souvenir of the Jubilee Year could have appeared.

Trustee-in-Trust, J. R. Walker, Heber J. Grant, John R. Park, W. S. Godbe, W. H. Rowe, M. H. Walker, John Sharp, Miriam Godbe Brooks, Geo. W. Thatcher, W. W. Chisholm, Moses Thatcher, J. F. Woodman, P. H. Lannan, Gill S. Peyton, T. G. Webber, George Romney, R. K. Thomas, Francis Armstrong, James Glendinning.

It scarcely needs intuition to foretell success for this little volume.

Byron Groo.

May, 1897.

*"Far in the West there lies a desert land,
    where the mountains
Lift, through perpetual snows, their lofty
    and luminous summits.
Where the gorge, like a gateway,
Opens a passage rude to the wheels of
    the emigrant's wagon."*

PLATES

	PAGE
NEBRASKA LANDSCAPE WITH A PRAIRIE FIRE	19
O'FALLEN'S BLUFFS ON THE PLATTE RIVER	20
A GATHERING STORM	22
COURT HOUSE ROCK	24
CHIMNEY ROCK	26
SCOTT'S BLUFFS	28
LEFT BY THE WAYSIDE	30
ABANDONED WAGONS AND CAMP MATERIAL	32
AMONG THE BLACK HILLS	34
LARAMIE PEAK	36
DISTANT VIEW OF THE RATTLESNAKE HILLS	38
DEVIL'S GATE	40
THE NIGHT GUARD	42
A BUFFALO HERD	44
ROCK INDEPENDENCE WIND RIVER MOUNTAINS, FROM HIGH SPRINGS	46
FORD OF THE GREEN RIVER	48
MOONLIGHT IN ECHO CANYON	50
GLIMPSE OF SALT LAKE VALLEY	52

DEDICATED TO THE MEMORY OF

MY FATHER.

The Old Journey

THIS old sketch book — well, well! How vividly it brings back those days—days gone this quarter; yes, nearer this half century! How unexpectedly we sometimes come upon the past—turn it up, as it were, from the mold of time, as with the plow one might bring to light from out the earth some lost and forgotten thing. This book, with its buckskin covers, revivifies dead hours; or, if not exactly that, brings them back in memory as reminders of times and conditions passed

THE OLD JOURNEY

away forever. The book received hard treatment in those days gone by, before it lay here so long gathering dust and cobwebs about it. It was never petted and taken care of, but was made to rough it in this world, so to speak, and to be treated with little consideration—made to withstand the brunt of many a hard encounter. Nor could its master have done otherwise for it had he so desired. Master and book were companions on a rough journey.

🌿 Inside and out the book shows its hard usage: the leaves and the covers all tell tales. This buckskin was drenched many a time by the thunder storms of Nebraska and Wyoming; between these sheets of variously-toned gray paper, close to the binding, are little waves of red, gritty stuff, contributions, on some windy day, from the sand-hills of the Platte Valley, or of the Big Sandy Creek (the poetic Glistening Gravel

THE OLD JOURNEY

Water of the Indians) or from the "Three Crossings," perhaps, or the weary bit of road leading over into Ash Hollow. One end of the book has been submerged in water, a reminiscence, no doubt, of the fording of either the Platte, the Sweetwater, the Laramie, or the Green River. O, there are all sorts of emotions revived by this book; they crowd upon me thick and fast! These crisp, gray leaves of sage—they got into it, I believe, one cool September night, at Quaking Asp Hollow, when great bonfires were blazing around the camp, and the red tongues of flame lit up with their light, wild groups of dancers—the ox-punchers performing strange antics; a fantastic dancing supposed to be under the patronage of Terpsichore; a something between that of our modern ball room and the Apache Ghost Dance.

✣ Yes, the book is a reminder, old, bat-

THE OLD JOURNEY

tered, dusty, yet truthful withal, of what an ox-team journey across the plains and over the Rockies was in the years that are gone.

❧ Turning the leaves it all comes back again. I go over the long, long plodding of seemingly endless days. Not only do I look upon the scenes which are shown in the book, but, through sympathy, on others also, that for want of time were left unsketched. Incidents of many kinds thrust their memories upon me. Sometimes the experiences recalled were pleasurable; sometimes they were sad. But mirthful or tragic, pathetic or humorous, I go over them again, and the twelve hundred miles, nay, the fifteen hundred, considering the circuitous route which we were compelled to follow, pass before me like a moving panorama. Prairies, hills, streams, mountains, canyons, follow each other in quick succession—all

THE OLD JOURNEY

the ever-changing prospect between the banks of the Missouri River and the Valley of the Great Salt Lake.

❧ How rapidly we have grown! What used to be dreams of the future first changed to reality, and then sank away until they are now but a dream of the past! No more the long train of dust-covered wagons, drawn by the slow and patient oxen, winds across the level plains or through the deep defile. No more the Pony Express or the lumbering stage coach brings the quickest word or forms the fastest transport between the inter-mountain region and "The States." How hard it is to understand the briefness of time that has passed since this great interior country was practically a howling wilderness, inhabited by bands of savage Indians and penetrated only by intrepid trappers or hunters! As we are now whirled along over the Laramie Plains, or through

THE OLD JOURNEY

the Echo and Weber Canyons, reclining on luxuriously-cushioned seats, and but a few hours away from the eastern seaboard, we can scarcely realize it. Surely the locomotive plays an important part in the destiny of modern nations! Without its aid the country through which we are about to pass might have become, as was surmised by Irving, the cradle of a race inimical to the higher civilization, to the East and the West. Now we behold it a land giving promise of future greatness, where peace, wealth and happiness shall go hand in hand, and where already it is well-nigh impossible for the youth of to-day to comprehend the struggles and privations of its pioneer fathers.

✣ Most of the sketches are roughly made. There was little time to loiter by the wayside. Some are hardly more than hasty outlines, filled in, perhaps, when the camp-

ing-ground was reached. Some show an impression dashed off of a morning or evening, or, sometimes, of a noonday. Once in a while there is a subject carefully finished, telling of an early camp, or of a half-day rest. Some are in black and white merely, others in color.

✤ The first sketch (near the Missouri River) shows a Nebraska landscape with a prairie fire sweeping across it. The scene is a very different one from what the place would present to-day; the great whirling mass of smoke, driven before the wind, and the principal feature of the sketch, overshadows with its darkness a far-reaching landscape of low, rolling hills, clumps of trees and a winding stream, in which, however, not a sign of life is visible. The stream is a small one, probably the Blue Creek, or it may be the Vermilion, or the Shell, perhaps. I have really forgotten which. Now that region is covered with farms and farm-houses, and the smoke which arises is from the chimneys of houses where prosperity dwells. The sketch shows a wilderness, so great is the change wrought since the day it was made.

❧ What a new delight it was, to one city-bred, to mingle in the freedom of camp-life such as we enjoyed near that spot, and how sweet, too, to pass his days and nights under the blue canopy of heaven! There was nothing very beautiful, certainly, in the scenery bordering on the "Mad Waters," but it was wild and sylvan at the time, and we were excited by the prospect of those months of travel before us. Eastward lay the river, with the steamer "Welcome" (which had brought us up the stream), the "Red Wing," and other old-time boats, passing occasionally up or down. Westward the level horizon attracted our eyes and

made us long for the hour when we should start to follow the setting sun.

❧ Persistently, and with eager curiosity, the guide-book, such as it was, was scanned. For weeks ahead we studied the route. We learned the names, suggestively odd or quaintly poetic, and pictured the places to which they belonged, forming conclusions to be realized later on, or to be dispelled by the actualities. The imagination, heated to the utmost by travelers' tales—half true, half false—looked forward to a region of romance. Before us was the land of Kit Carson; of the Sioux, the Cheyenne, and the Ute. In our path was the home of the prairie dog, the coyote, and the rattle-snake; of the antelope, the buffalo, and the bear.

❧ But I am forgetting the sketches. Next in the book is a quick rubbing-in of the O'Fallen's Bluffs. The sky and the river— the slow-flowing Platte—are responsive to the light of a golden sunset. The brilliant rays radiate from behind the huge, square bluffs which throw a shadow across the foreground. The main interest in the scene, however, from our present standpoint, is the train of wagons winding along the dusty road.

🙦 And so we had made a start! We had unraveled the mysteries attendant upon the management of cattle; could yoke and unyoke; knew the effects of "gee" and "haw" and could throw four yards of blacksnake whip with a force that made its buckskin "cracker" explode with a noise like the report of a pistol.

🙦 Dearly we learned to love the Platte! Even if the way was dreary at times we forgot it when traveling beside its banks. "Egypt, O Commander of the faithful, is a compound of black earth and green plants, between a pulverized mountain and a red

THE OLD JOURNEY

sand." So said Amrou, Conqueror of Egypt, to his master, the Khalif Omar, and so almost might we have said of the Valley of the Platte. Day after day we trudged along, and day after day the red hills of sandstone looked down upon us. The days grew into weeks, the weeks became a month, and still the cattle, freed from the yoke, hastened to slake their thirst at the stream. During that month we ate, each of us, that peck of dirt—if sand may be classed as dirt—which every man is said to eat in his lifetime. To the overland traveler of today, the Platte is almost unknown; but from the time we first discerned the stream, yellowed in the close of a July day and overhung by ancient cottonwood trees, until we bade it adieu at Red Rocks, within view of Laramie Peak, it seemed as a friend. As on the edge of the Nile, the verdure on its banks was often the only greenness in all the landscape round.

THE OLD JOURNEY

❧ What possible enjoyment is there in the long and dreary ride over the yellow plains?" Rideing, in his "Scenery of the Pacific Railway," asks the question. "The infinite breadth of space and air does not redeem the dismal prospect of dried-up seas." "The pleasures of the trans-continental journey," he goes on to say, "may be divided into ten parts, five of which consist of anticipation, one of realization, and four of retrospect." With us, at least, it was different. From the railway one is but a beholder of the scenery; but in the old journey we were partakers therein. We became acquainted with the individualities of the way. One there was in our company who, like Phil Robinson, of travel'd fame, remembered the principal places along the road by the game he had shot there. Here he had dropped a mallard, and there a red-head; on the banks of that stream he had

brought down a deer, and on that plain had ridden down a buffalo; a good way to remember, perhaps, but unlike him I recall all the good spots for bathing. O, what joy it was after a day of toil to plunge into the cooling waters of the Platte.! Now I see sparkling, the waves of the Elkhorn; now it is those of the Little Laramie; and now, through a fringe of long-leaved arrow-wood, the cold, deep waters of the Horse-Shoe Creek. One day as I bathed, Spotted Tail, the famous Sioux Chieftain, and his band of five hundred braves, passed along on the banks of the Platte. Open mouthed I stared and while wading ashore, I struck my foot against (as it proved to be on examination) a great stone battle-axe. Perhaps it once belonged at some remote period of time, to another chief in that warrior's ancestry.

⚜ "A Gathering Storm"—the unbroken

THE OLD JOURNEY

prairie. We are brought by these to grand phenomena. Heavens, what piles of cloud! What solemn loneliness!

> "Gloomy and dark art thou, O chief of the mighty Omahas;
> Gloomy and dark as the driving cloud, whose name thou hast taken."

✱ The words of Longfellow come quickly to the lips. These prairies may not be as beautiful as those of which he and Bryant sang—they were farther to the south, I imagine — but they were fair enough. Though not

> "Bright with luxuriant clusters of roses and purple amorphas,"

nor covered with

> "Billowy bays of grass ever rolling in shadow and sunshine;"

THE OLD JOURNEY

yet under the spell of magnificent cloud scenery they were grand and dramatic.

☙ Here are two famous objects; famous, at least, in those days—not far apart and following each other in the book—"The Court House," and the "Chimney Rock." Distinctly I remember the day on which we first sighted the latter—a pale, blue shaft above the plain. We had just formed our noon corral, and through its western opening we saw the chimney, wavy through the haze which arose from the heated ground. It seemed to us that the slow-going oxen would never reach it; or rather, that they would never come to the point in the road opposite that natural curiosity, for the emigrant road passed several miles to the northward of the low range of bluffs of which the "Chimney" is a part. From the banks of Lawrence Creek, where the sketch was made, the bluffs are most picturesque. Strings of wild duck arose from the rushes as our train approached on its way.

✣ "Scott's Bluffs" make a very different picture from those of O'Fallen. The sedimentary heights of the former, with their strong resemblance to walls and towers, are rosy with the light of the rising sun. In the middle distance, in a little valley, is the train corralled, the steel-blue smoke rising in a straight column from the morning camp-fires. In the foreground are sunflowers, a buffalo skull among them.

✣ Ah! here is a sad, dark sketch—"Left by the Roadside." The tall, rank growth and a low, half-sunken head-board are dark against the sky in which lingers yet a red flush of the twilight. Two or three stars shed their paly rays from afar, and one feels that the silence is unbroken by even the faintest sigh of wind. But certainly

there will come one soon, a long, shivering, almost moan-like sound, as the wind creeps stealthily across the waste and gently stirs the prairie grass and flowers.

⚘ Countless in numbers almost were those silent witnesses of death by the way. The mounds were to be seen in all imaginable places. Each day we passed them, singly or in groups; and sometimes, nay, often, one of our own company was left behind to swell the number. By the banks of streams, on grassy hillocks, in the sands, beneath groves of trees, or among piles of rock, the graves were dug. We left the new mounds to be beaten upon by the tempests, scorched by the sun or for beauty to gather about as it had about many of the older ones. Sometimes where we camped the old graves would be directly alongside the wagons. I recall sitting by one that was thickly covered with grass and without a head-

THE OLD JOURNEY

board while I ate my evening meal, and of sleeping beside it at night. One remains in my mind as a very soothing little picture—a child's grave, and it was screened around with a thicket of wild rose that leaned lovingly over it, while the mound itself was overgrown with moss. I fancied that the parents of that child, were they yet living, would like to have seen how daintily nature had decked the last bed of their loved one.

How painful were the circumstances attending the first burial in our train. A woman died one evening (we were about ten days out) just as the moon had risen over the prairie, and swiftly the tidings sped through the camp. Next morning (it was the Sabbath Day) she was buried—laid to rest on a low grassy hill near a stream. Never can I forget the grief of her children as the body was lowered into the ground. A network of stakes was placed across the

THE OLD JOURNEY

grave to keep away the robber wolves, and a hymn was then sung, accompanied by the plaintive wailing of a clarionet.

❧ That first death made a sad impression on our company, but after a while the burials became so frequent that they lost much of their saddening power; or, rather, we refused to retain the sadness, throwing it off in self-defence.

❧ The outline which follows brings up a different train of thought—"Camp material abandoned after an attack by Indians." The ground is littered with all sorts of indescribable things. Panic is evident in the reckless tossing away of every kind of article, anything to lighten the loads so that the fear-struck emigrants could hurry forward. This was the train immediately preceding ours, and a couple of days later we passed one of those prairie letters—an ox shoulder-blade—on which was written:

THE OLD JOURNEY

"Captain ———— train passed here
August 14th, 18—
8 deaths.
90 head of cattle driven away by the Indians.
Great scare in Camp."

❧ Apropos of alarms from the Indians there is a rapidly executed subject (from memory next day) that brings back a night of peril and sorrow. It was on the western slope of the Black Hills and there were five wagons of us belated from the general train. We were the last five on the right wing and the right wing was the latter half of the train that night, so, practically we were alone. There was a dead woman in one of the wagons, and to hear the weeping and sobbing of her little children, in the dark beside the corpse, was heart-chilling.

THE OLD JOURNEY

The poor husband trudged along on foot, hurrying his single yoke of footsore cattle. Still we were far behind; liable at any moment to be cut off by the prowling Sioux. That was a night to remember.

✤ Here are two scenes among the Black Hills themselves, one a very suggestive sketch showing rocks, timber-clad bluffs, and ragged peaks with the wagons of the train coming down a steep declivity into a dry torrent bed. Wild clouds are coming over the peaks threatening a stormy night. It appears that the wagons must topple over, end over end, so abrupt is the descent they are making. In the other sketch, made on the evening of the second day following, the train is seen winding like a serpent over the hills. In the middle distance is a valley partly obscured by mists and beyond it stands Laramie Peak, purple against the sunset clouds and sky.

THE OLD JOURNEY

❧ The night drives were among the most trying experiences upon the overland journey. Usually they resulted from the drying of some stream or spring where we had expected to make the evening camp, and the consequent necessity of moving forward. Our worst drive of this kind was to reach La Prelle River after leaving Fort Laramie, on the night which followed the making of the first of the two sketches just mentioned. Wildly the lightnings glared, their lurid tongues licking the ground beside us. The road was deluged in the downpour of water; and what with the crashing of thunder, the sudden glare of light, and the wild dashing of rain, the poor cattle were quite panic-stricken. It was hard work to make the poor brutes face the storm. Yet, after all, their sagacity was better than ours. Several times we would have driven them over the edge of a

THE OLD JOURNEY

precipice had not their keener senses warned them back. We would have shuddered, so our captain afterwards told us, could we have seen where the tracks of our wagon-wheels were made that night.

    I try to recall my diary (I did keep a diary, though long since it was fed to the flames.) It must have contained some interesting pages about this part of the journey, though I cannot recall a word. The events which gave rise to its entries are fresh in my mind, but the matter itself has gone. There was something in it about Scott's Bluffs, and how they received their name— one fancied that he could see the wounded trapper, abandoned and dying alone, and wondered if he crawled down from the bluffs and along by the way we were traveling to the spot where, at last, his bones were found. There was something, too, about the gathering of buffalo chips and

THE OLD JOURNEY

the seeking of firewood. What lonely spots we did visit! One comes to my mind at this instant. How sadly the wind quired in the ancient cedars, and how very old appeared the boulders with their mottling of lichens and with what a dismal yelp a ragged coyote leaped from his lair and scampered down a rock-stream gully! It was tantalizing at times to keep to the road. How could one resist the temptation to throw off restraint, and putting all prudence aside leap on horse-back and go galloping away over hill and through dale? What if the redman did lie in the way? He could be a brother. O, but to be like him; to live wild and free, to be "iron-jointed, supple-sinew'd, to hurl our lances in the sun!"

✣ This, of course, was on those days when having taken "the winds and sunshine into our veins," we felt stirred within us the instincts of primal man. At other times

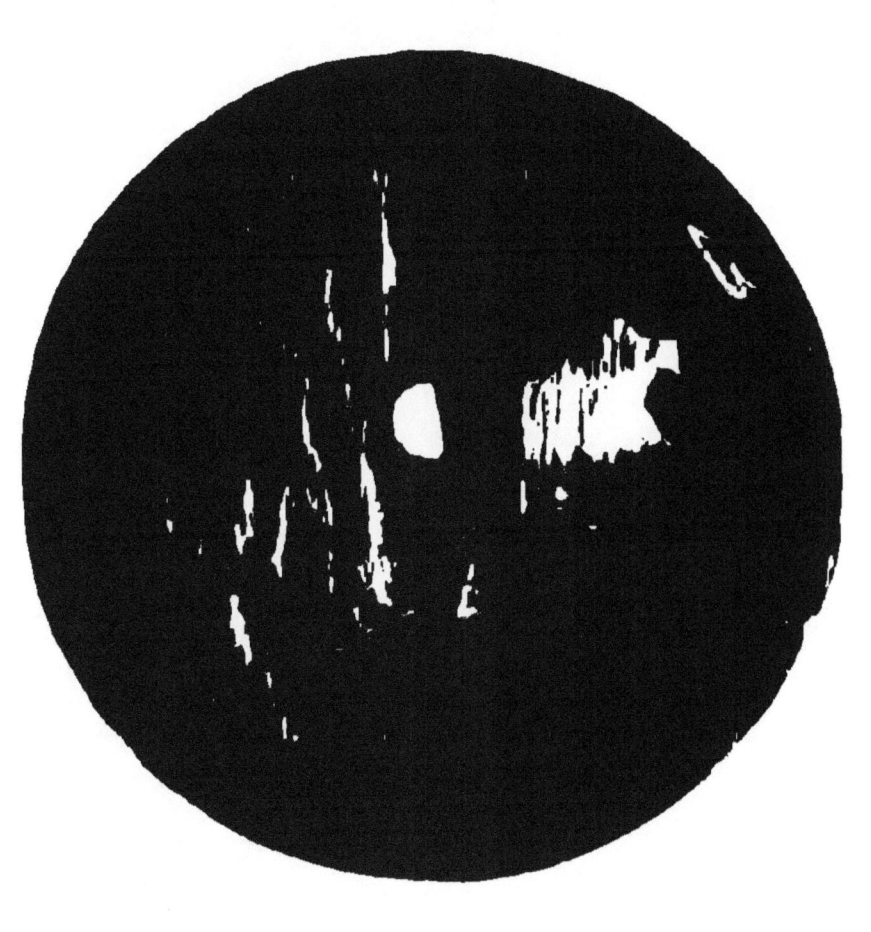

we were sober-minded enough. The romance of being out in the wilds was terribly chilled by an inclement sky. A few days of drizzling rain tried the most ardent spirit. Then it was that the disagreeableness of the time made the true mettle of the emigrant show itself. Whatever traits of character he possessed—selfishness, senseless fault-finding, or those rarer qualities of kindness, cheerful content, and ready helpfulness—all came out. In Mark Tapley's own phrase, it was all very well to "come out strong" when by the warm glow of the flames, or when moving along with the bright blue sky above us, but it was quite a different task to remain cheerful when the incessant rain made impossible even the smallest of camp-fires, and one crept to bed with wet clothes and chilled to the bone, without even the solace of a cup of hot coffee.

THE OLD JOURNEY

❦ Hardly less trying were the days of duststorms. What a misery it was when the wind blew from the front, and the whole cloud of dust raised by the motion of seventy-five wagons and over three hundred yoke of cattle, drove in our faces. How intolerably our eyes and our nostrils burned, and how quickly our ears were filled with the flying sand.

❦ Here is a suggestion of a sometimes unpleasant duty. "The Night Guard." His was a trust in which labor, anxiety and danger were often combined. The picket on duty at the front of war was scarcely more important than he. In those days of lawlessness, in red man and white, constant vigil had to be kept. On the faithful performance of the night guard's duty, our safety depended. Alone with his thoughts, too, he had ample opportunity for careful reflection. Men who can now count their wealth

THE OLD JOURNEY

by hundreds of thousands, some by the millions of dollars, can remember their vain strivings when poor and on night guard to look into the future; to see some faint glimpse of what fortune held in store for them in the "Westward Ho!"

✣ We, like ships that pass on the sea, sometimes spoke a returner. No gloomy recital of disappointment could turn us back. The Golden West was our goal and those who returned were but, to us, the too timid ones. In truth, has not the dream of the Pioneer been fully realized?

✣ Three subjects that follow are by the Sweetwater River. In one the Rattlesnake Hills are shown, dim in the summer haze, and in the second is the "Rock Independence;" in the third is the noted "Devil's Gate," with its reflection in a pool of the stream.

✣ Irving, in his Bonneville, describes "A

THE OLD JOURNEY

Buffalo Herd." When seen at a distance "they resemble a grove of low, thick-set trees." On a distant plain or along a hillside they might easily be mistaken for clustered scrub-oak. Ash Hollow was once a favorite resort of the now rare animal. A traveler once saw there a herd which could scarcely have numbered less than from fifty to sixty thousand. So vast were the herds in the valley of the upper Platte, that it would sometimes take several days for one of them to pass a given point. Woe to the small party of emigrants that happened to be in the track of such a herd of frightened buffaloes!

❧ Scarcely less dangerous was a stampede of cattle. Helter-skelter, maddened by fear, blind as their wild fellows, the stupid creatures rushed recklessly on. No longer the patient, submissive beasts whose pace seemed ever too slow to our eager desires, but full

THE OLD JOURNEY

of fury, dashing they cared not where. A stampede of yoked cattle was one of our most lively episodes.

❧ Here is a wide gap in the locale of sketches—the result of a mountain fever. What a gloriously majestic outline the peaks of the Wind River Mountains make, and especially from this spot—the High Springs, in the South Pass! Delightsome days were ours, as we moved slowly forward through that broad highway, with those towering mountains all the while seeming to gaze down upon us! Joyfully we burst into song:

> "All hail ye snow-capped mountains!
> Golden sunbeams smile."

❧ And what a time of gaiety, too, followed each day's drive, when the evening

THE OLD JOURNEY

meal was over and the sweet-toned clarionet assembled all in the open corral, and the young men and women, and the older ones, too, danced the hours away, forgetful in the merriment of the time, of the fatigues that were past and those that were to come. It was such hours as these that atoned for those which had been sad.

That clarionet, what an important part it held! It voiced the general feeling of the train.

♪ Merrily, on the banks of the Missouri, sounded its notes at the moment of starting. Mournfully it spoke as each one who fell by

the wayside was laid away to his rest. I seem to hear it once again as when we reached the Chimney Rock—the half-way house it was sometimes called—and all gave themselves up to unbounded jollity, and as it awoke us, too, for the last start near our journey's end. Its remembered strains bring back the scent of prairie flowers and the homely sage.

❧ But this reviewing grows lengthy, and now we are nearing the end. Small need to tell how expectancy grew upon us as the number of miles ahead grew less and less. Even those who had apparently grown apathetic and trudged silently along, or sat questionless in the wagons, began to manifest the same eager interest which had marked the days of our starting out. Wake up! wake up! wake up! Fun and frolic must sometimes take the place of sentiment and sobriety, and so one who was ever brimming over with both could not wait the poetic summons of the clarionet. Beating together two old tin pans he frisked around the corral, rousing with the unseemly noise all laggards and slug-a-beds.

❧ Here is the "Ford of the Green River," not where the railway crosses it at the present day, but farther up the stream, where in the distance, the north-east, the jagged summits of the Wind River Mountains were again in view, and where on the river banks are groups of Cottonwood trees and thickets of wild raspberry and rose, and the air is aromatic with the exhalations of wild thyme. It is a stirring scene, for the water was deep and swift and the fording not accomplished wilhout danger. A half-day's rest on the banks of Green River, as well as the attractiveness of the place itself, makes the scene of that sketch remembered with pleasure.

THE OLD JOURNEY

✣ "Echo Canyon" brings us within the borders of Utah. Clear shone the September sun, as our long train wound slowly under the conglomerate cliffs; slowly, for half the cattle were footsore, and all way-weary. Several hours were consumed in passing through the defile, and night was falling ere the mouth of the canyon was reached. Later, as the camp-fires were blazing, the full moon illumined the fantastic scene.

✣ Who of all those that traversed Echo Canyon in an ox-team train will forget the shouting, the cracking of whips, the wild halloas, and the pistol-shots that resounded along the line, or the echoes, all confused by the multitude of sounds, and passing through each other like the concentric rings on a still pond when we throw in a handful of pebbles, flying from cliff to cliff and away up in the shaggy ravines and seeming to come back at last from the sky?

"O hark, O hear! how thin and clear,
  And thinner, clearer, farther going!
O sweet and far from cliff and scar
  The horns of Elfland faintly blowing!
Blow, let us hear the purple glens replying;
Blow, bugle, answer, echoes, dying, dying,
  dying."

❧ No wonder the place recalls Tennyson's song, but, it must be told, there were none of "the horns of Elfland faintly blowing" about the wild hilarity of sounds which were sent back from the cliffs that day.

❧ The last sketch in the book is a "Glimpse of the Valley." Not one in our company but what felt the heart swell with joy as the sight of fields and orchards, in which hung ripened fruit, burst upon our

THE OLD JOURNEY

sight. Danger and fatigues were all forgotten. The stubborn interminable miles were conquered, "The Journey" was at an end.

www.ingramcontent.com/pod-product-compliance
Lightning Source LLC
Chambersburg PA
CBHW031607110426
42742CB00037B/1313